DECODING HATE

The Only Cure is Understanding

CLARENCE KD McNAIR

ISBN-13: 978-1-954609-28-0

This book was printed in the United States of America

For information regarding special discounts for bulk purchases, please contact the publisher:

LaBoo Publishing Enterprise, LLC
staff@laboopublishing.com
www.laboopublishing.com

Connect with the author on all social media @clarencekdmcnair

TABLE OF CONTENTS

ACKNOWLEDGMENTS

I would like to thank my readers first. This book is dedicated to you. I hope this book transforms minds from negative thoughts. Thank you for seeing my work as a tool for change and understanding. I'd like to thank life for what it has taught me. We all have experienced some kind of unfair judgment or treatment for many different reasons. It's called life, the good the bad and the ugly. However, there is always a solution. Everyone who picks up this book can be a part of breaking the walls down one reader at a time. A special dedication to all the nonprofits and community support groups and organizations who work day-to-day for change to create a NO Hate Zone. I'm so grateful for every contribution that helps the world. Also, I dedicate this book to all the teachers around the world and to the YouTubers and social media platform users who commit every day to bring awareness and understanding. Every day, someone's life and perspective is impacted by your positive work, so thank you. To the man in the mirror, all around the world, there is more to life than what you see. All you have to do is put in the work.

SPECIAL THANKS

A special thank you to the McNair books family. To the women who helped me bring my gift to life, Kimmoly K. LaBoo, thank you: you're a gift from GOD. Kristina Brooks, your knowledge is priceless. Shout out to everyone in the world who takes the time to work on themselves. You understand that talk is cheap, and action moves us forward. We can no longer accept people for who they are if who they are is destroying other people's lives and hurting people around them and in their life. So thank you: thanks to everyone who puts in the work to make the world a better place.

INTRODUCTION
A MESSAGE TO THE HATERS

You are valuable, you have worth, and you are also one of God's children. Never feel like someone else doesn't deserve what you don't have. Just because it appears they have a perfect life with all of the blessings, material belongings, accolades, and attention, remember, there are conversations all of us have individually that no one knows about. Those conversations are between you and God. Even if you don't believe in God, there are moments when you are in the room by yourself with no makeup, no jewelry, no clothes... nothing, just you being face to face with yourself. Only you know those battles within. When you look at what other people have, remember that you don't know what battles that person faced. Maybe they've done a good job of covering it up. Just because someone has what looks like a perfect life doesn't mean they are perfect. You shouldn't judge a person or develop ill feelings towards them, when you don't know what they have going on internally. You don't know what in the hell they had to overcome. You don't know what in the hell they are feeling and still facing. There's something very valuable that you have that no one else can take away from you, and that's who you are. No one can be duplicated; you are the original. There's only one you. You can never be somebody else, and that somebody can never be you. That's what makes you special. We will know the journey that person endured and the decisions they had to come face to face with. They were either going to quit and fall victim to the obstacle, or they were going to keep going.

I wrote this book ***Decoding Hate*** because I wanted people to know that there is no solution without understanding. In life, sometimes we have to step back and stop being envious of what we see other people with. There are some people who don't get any sleep at night because they have to work two or three jobs. There are people that have to be on the road traveling all the time away from their family and loved ones. You may see them with jewelry or cars, but are you willing to sacrifice the same in order to get where they are? Are you willing to not go out on the weekends and take the money you have to invest into yourself? Even if it's five dollars. Maybe that money can get you a haircut to make you feel better about yourself, so you can get in front of the right people. Have you tried to network, go to job fairs, sit in a room with other people who are where you want to be? Even if you can't get into the room with celebrities or professionals like doctors and lawyers or highly educated people, have you tried to get in a circle of people who just want better for themselves? You could be working at McDonald's or Chick-fil-a to help you get one level above where you are. Instead, you're on social media looking at other people flying on private jets, owning fancy cars, and wearing expensive clothes. In the back of your mind, you start to have those negative thoughts and are envious of people without knowing their journey. If you want to get to know the person, then read up on them if it's available, since you're that obsessed with them, and think they're a god. Maybe you should snap out of your emotions and get back to reality. You don't know the pressure, responsibilities, and burdens this person carries. If you had to trade shoes with this person, could you even stand or walk in them for a minute? Or are you running around trying to hand everybody your shoes so that you don't have to walk in them? Are your shoes even worth trading? It's time to be realistic and understand those shoes may carry a lot of pain, frustration, and moments of triumph to overcome obstacles. So, for every hater out there that's watching people on social media, reading the blogs on influencers, watching TV every day, sitting at home watching them pull up to their houses with shopping bags from the mall, make sure you study the grind as well. Oftentimes, people don't see successful people going to work at 3 a.m., or the consistent trips to UPS to drop off packages, or the amount of sleep they lose trying to take care of their family. The haters see them dressed up on the weekends on social media, but don't see that 9–5 grind. They don't see the overtime you put in just to buy those shoes or that purse. They are jealous of the outcomes but overlook the work you dedicated to your goals. For all the haters choosing to walk in their misery, there is help available. There are psychologists, books like this, and resources out there to enhance your way of thinking. You don't have to stay in your hate. You don't have to feel like there's never a chance for you to make it. You have to know that your time will come, but you have to be humble and let somebody help you. This book is for us to use as daily maintenance for our lives. You have to realize this is a journey. You can't wake up tomorrow and be complete. We all have challenges that arise and make us want to give up. You have to find something that motivates you. Maybe you want to give your family better. Maybe you don't have talent, but you have responsibilities that make you want to do special things for the people you love. I hope this book touches you in a place where it changes your life.

It was the year 2017, as I was jogging around the lake, that a thought came across my mind. I began to look around and notice how the people around me all had one thing in common: We are the only creation that doesn't need to be plugged into anything in order to function. We're the only species where our bodies have the ability to rest while our hearts work at the same time. We are all known as human beings with a commonality to be in the world as individuals, while our experiences shape how we see life from a different perspective. I thought to myself, "What if everyone understood each other? What if everyone had a moment to express themselves? What if there was no media or television? What if everyone was on the same page?" Unfortunately, that's not our reality anymore. The truth is: there is hate amongst and hatred towards one another in this world. All these thoughts in my mind made me wish everybody could just love each other. I question why there is so much separation in this world. It was time for us to decode this hatred and look closer into where the perception of hate comes from. The concept of writing a book called **Decoding Hate** came to mind to raise awareness and give some understanding as to *why* people hate. It's time to get a better understanding based on my viewpoint, along with receiving advice on how people can communicate better, interact more, and eliminate their barriers. I wanted to write this book to dig deeper into one of the biggest problems known to man: the mystery of hate. In this book, we will discuss social media and how the influencer community cultivates hate based on the new digital age we live in. I will look into why some people receive love on social media, and why others can't seem to break the ice in the social media space. I'm sure everyone has experienced some sort of hatred towards them or have been judged based on their own perception of a person. Everyone has dealt with someone who disliked them. While all of these thoughts raced through my mind in 2017, I knew it would take time to develop this concept. I had no idea of when I would complete this project, but I give thanks to the pandemic because it allowed me to create something to benefit others instead of dwelling on the sorrows taking place. I used the time when we could not interact with each other to be creative so I could eventually help others. While there could be a million reasons why people hate, I'm going to explain the ones I figured out. After all, a little bit of information, insight, and understanding goes a long way.

Hate: to feel intense or passionate dislike for (someone).

Some people are jealous of the outcomes you have achieved because they don't know your story. They don't understand your journey nor all you've dealt with to overcome what you came from, in order to get to where you are. If you look at social media, the people with the most love and respect are most open and real about their experiences to their followers. They communicate well and live their truth. Think about this: if I post nice things all day and have no communication with my followers, they will see me and make their own opinion of me because I never shared anything about me personally. You have to talk about your journey—not just the good things, but the dark side no one likes to talk about. There are many reasons why people exude hate onto you. I realize mankind envies what they don't understand, but the love comes from people connecting to your story. At the end of the day, everything is about people feeling like they see themselves in you. Sometimes there are people we look up to because they give us hope. We feel connected to them in some way, shape or form. I remember speaking at my class reunion where there were people who've known me for years. However, they never knew everything I went through. I shared my story, and everyone was stirred up or in tears. They kept coming up to me to give me hugs after sharing my truth because now they understood me. I painted the picture of how hard and long of a journey it was for me to become who I am today.

CHAPTER 1
THE POWER OF EXPRESSION

Communication is the act of giving, receiving, and sharing information—in other words, talking or writing, and listening or reading. Good communicators listen carefully, speak or write clearly, and respect different opinions (commonsensemedia.org). When you want to break the ice and get through to someone, it is very important for you to understand their communication. It can change the room and the world around you. After the release of my first book, I noticed a huge change in how people connected with me. Their perception of me changed once I wrote about my personal story. Even the people who may not have liked me gained respect for me because they understood me after reading my book.

Expression is the process of making one's thoughts or feelings known. In this world, we have the ability to express ourselves. Unfortunately, we live in a world that lacks expression. When you express your feelings and your emotions, you create an open door for people to come inside your thoughts, which creates a better understanding of who you are. Your feelings give people perspective to connect with you and not be so quick to judge you. Charles Wright had a song called "Express Yourself." That song is more powerful than many people realize. It's important to release those thoughts of expression within. People fail to realize that expressions create personalities. There are so many feelings and thoughts you've been holding in, to the point where these feelings and thoughts start to manifest through your personality and your physical vibe. Everyone expresses themselves in many different ways. Some express themselves through crying, violence, fighting, or arguing. Some people get angry and stop being kind to other people because they feel they've been taken advantage of, or are misunderstood, or not appreciated. When a person does not have anyone to talk to or they are neglected during very vulnerable times of their life, it can transform their mentality into hate and make them develop a negative perspective on life. The big question is: why do people hate? Many people have been muted since childhood, never being able to express themselves and their true power. While the lack of expression can have a very negative outcome, a positive expression can have a life-changing outcome not only in your personal life, but in society. In the world around us, we have turned into robots – lacking empathy, lacking emotions, lacking understanding. We've turned a mute ear to people who cannot offer us anything or satisfy our personal needs and desires. We live in a world that instantly turns the communication off to people who simply need someone to talk to. Those people who are shut out then become cold-hearted and start to project hateful energy. People say this person is a horrible person, but that's not always the case. We have to start being realistic. If you don't open up and connect with people, then those people will not be able to connect with you.

CHAPTER 2
YOUR STORY CHANGES HEARTS

One thing's for sure, so many stories go unheard. Can you imagine the millions of people walking around every single day with so much buried inside of them? You could be around someone for many years who experienced a tragedy that they never saw coming. They try to be so strong during that time. If people would open up and talk about those tragedies, they would be able to release and understand how to connect. There is nothing new under the sun. We all have experienced challenges in life that put us in situations where we took on more than we could handle mentally. Everyone can relate, because we all overwork ourselves and do too much alone without knowing how to ask for help. We convinced ourselves no one would help us and that what's inside of us is so different than what has ever happened to anyone before in the world. The biggest one we are always worried about is what other people will think about us. We care so much about what they think that it consumes our entire life.

We become a hostage to our own thoughts, emotions, fears, insecurities, and problems. Then, we create false perspectives, believing that if people know too much, then they will have power over us, won't love us, they won't see us the same way, or we won't have any friends. You begin to think no one will root for you, so you put these walls up and live a double life. You become a smiling face on the outside with brokenness and hurt on the inside. We all want someone to listen. You just have to open up and know that your story will change hearts. Your truth can literally set you free. Without open conversations, there is no room to grow. Your problems will never be solved, differences will never be ironed out, disagreements will never be explained, understanding will never arise. Through your journey, by revealing the truth we start to build emotional connections with others and begin changing the hearts of others.

CHAPTER 3
DEAR EMOTIONS

Never judge a book by its cover, because there are so many pages on the inside that the world should know. We walk around not realizing everyone has a story under their outer appearance. You have to be really careful of how you deal with people, because you just never know what's on the inside. You never know at what point that person may break or that person may hit the point of no return. It's very wise to definitely treat people the way you want to be treated. Most importantly, you have to live with compassion and understand that everyone has gone through something in life you may not know about. Everyone has something special on the inside and may be experiencing a lot of doubt, fear, anxiety, and regret. You could just be that person who unburies them from six feet of negative energy, negative experiences, and a negative lifestyle. You set them free by reading the many pages inside of them. Unfortunately, some people's internal genius never makes it to their lips before killing someone.

There are so many potential great contributions in the world that simply never get heard. I really hope that after reading this book, you receive this message. If you are a person who battles and struggles with negative emotions towards others, I hope this book brings awareness to the reality of actions and helps you to understand how everything is much deeper than what your eyes can see. Accept the fact that everyone on this planet has gone through something. You may not be where they are at this time in your life, but it does not mean that your time will not come. Why waste negative energy being jealous, having animosity and hatred toward someone? Take this time to work on yourself and focus on your time for growth. Your turn for success will come, so be a blessing in this moment. Learn how to be understanding towards others. By not judging a book by its cover, we can begin to change the world and focus on the story within them. If you dwell on the title and outer appearance of a person, you'll miss the whole point of the book. My goal is not to be so deep, but to get straight to the point. So before you hate a person based on what you see or hear, just remember no one is perfect or was given a perfect life. You'll never really know the road that person has to travel. You see them in their light and in their success, but don't forget: everything that shines was dark at some point.

CHAPTER 4
STOP HIDING EVERYTHING, YOU WILL PAY LATER

Some people keep everything to themselves: their pain, their hurt, their happiness, their wins, their business. If you never talk and express anything, you will pay in the end. We live in a world that's full of judgment. Every day, people die with no one ever understanding them. It's cool to keep things quiet. However, you have to stop being selfish, open up and share at some point. You never know whose life you will change, so start sharing what's behind the shiny things. Remember, people look, listen, then judge what you are showing and saying to them. The biggest example of communication is music. Do you think Jay Z would have become so big of an artist if we did not know his story? I believe he would not have so many fans if he didn't share his story. Many people can connect with his story and see themselves in him. When people can relate to you, the hate goes out the door, because it allows people of like minds, stories, and beliefs to come together and help fight for what they believe in. It works because they are all on the same page together. They do not hate one another because they see each other equally. There's no hate present amongst them because they feel they are all one. Recently, there was an incident of a rapper who said something offensive to a community of people. It was not his words that hurt them, but rather that he did not know what they went through in their journey. So, when they heard him make those comments, the pain was in their truth, and all they had to fight for based on what they believed in. They try to get people to not judge them and seek to understand them. It's the same thing in a romantic relationship. If you get into a disagreement with your partner and they say the wrong thing, it will make you go off. Imagine someone opening the door to all of your ups and downs. You will feel more judgmental, which then creates more problems. How many times have we heard someone say, "If only they understood me?" People judge what they don't understand, so before you exude hate on someone, always remember to treat people with love and respect. When we block the need to understand others, we can never truly be happy for anyone. In order to understand others, you must look at life and accept that all people are different. This is the key to setting all of us free.

CHAPTER 5
WHY PEOPLE DO WHAT THEY DO

What are your thoughts attached to? Have you ever wondered why you think the way you think? Have you ever wondered where those thoughts come from? They say "Time heals all wounds," but that is not true. As time goes, we get better at hiding those things that have attached themselves to us. Whether through childhood or adult life, your thoughts and perception and thoughts of people are a reflection of your thoughts being attached to something more, an experience or trauma. Many of us believe that actions speak louder than words. The truth is, words speak louder than actions. Those are the words that we hear then believe in our minds. There's a million and one reasons as to why people do what they do. Those actions relate to how people receive something that is shown as celebration and positivity. A person who suffers with a mindset of hatred can never appreciate a person, because they see life from a negative lens. If I put on nice clothes, cologne, smell and look good, go wash my car and feel great, to someone else that could come off as being arrogant, based on how they perceive what they see, not realizing it's absolutely normal for a person to love themselves enough to want to dress up, celebrate, and enjoy life and the fruits of their hard work. When people have challenges and overcome those challenges, people want to enjoy all of the things they worked hard for. However, other people may see it as a threat, as if you are taking something away from them. Those people may feel like you're taking the attention away from them. You are now competition, or they think you're being offensive because you choose to live and enjoy your life. This is another reason why people might hate you when they don't even know you. Society has created a picture in their minds of misinformation to embed hatred into their thoughts if a person looks a certain way or has a certain lifestyle. Some may even do the opposite and love them just for having a different lifestyle. We even learn that if someone has less, then it's okay to not treat them with the same respect as a person who has more. Society and the media sometimes create these stereotypes or guidelines on how to treat people in life. These guidelines may resemble: If you have money and status, then everyone should bow down to you. If you don't have these things and you're just a person getting by, then we should give you the cold shoulder or pay you no attention. If you are a woman and you don't have a nice shape, then you're not someone who should be an influencer – as if a person's shape determines their ability to influence people. Everything has been microwaved and watered down to the point that we have more people suffering from lack of loving themselves because the world teaches you to hate yourselves. So not only are we dealing with people who hate others, but we are also dealing with people who hate themselves. It's all because of society, media, television, and music that we don't love our flaws anymore. We don't love the imperfections that make us human. We start to hate those things that make us human, as if everything has to be perfect. We've convinced ourselves that life is perfect when it's not. We start to hate the natural self and take on a robotic form in an attempt to preprogram every single step and move. We become politically correct without free-flowing human speech. Everything is strategic and edited, which fuels hate towards ourselves. It makes people believe that if you want to be loved and liked by everyone, then you have to replace yourself with a false version of yourself.

Clarence KD McNair

CHAPTER 6
PAIN & STRUGGLE ARE THE GREATEST CONNECTORS

Pain and struggle are the greatest connectors because at some point we will all endure one or the other. Whether emotional or physical, being let down or having a broken heart, a relationship going bad, or having frustration from denial; this is what pain is. Whereas struggle is what you endure, such as trying to find a career or increase your finances, trying to overcome something such as an addiction, or struggling to make decisions. These are all things we will encounter at some point. These are great connectors because we can relate to those two words: pain and struggle. So when people share their pain and struggle stories, it creates an open door for communication, because it's something we all can relate to. It gives the person sharing and the listener an instant connection and a desire to see that person succeed in life, because we feel as though they paid their dues. The necessary struggle they were able to overcome gives us a sense of sympathy for those who had to go through the pain and struggles to get to where they are. It's those certain situations that expose the toughness of life and allows people to connect through these two experiences.

CHAPTER 7
THE TRUTH IS WHAT IT IS

People hate the truth. Not the truth from science and research. Not the truth from studying out of a textbook. It's the truth of who you truly are internally. We get it mixed up when we live by facts and scientific research or when things are according to the statistics. All of those outlets say this and that about people based on their background. However, when people truly discover themselves and start to walk in their truth, they will find that some people will not agree with their truth. We live in a world where we have tried to normalize a person being one way, but when you're different, people judge you. Now, this is not to say my way of life or your way of life is any better, but there are public standards on who you can be, and if you become someone different, then yes, they judge you. Just remember this: it is better to be judged for who you truly are, than to be judged for being who you are not.

CHAPTER 8
A WORLD WITH UNDERSTANDING

You must understand that even your enemy falls on hard times. No matter who you are, everyone needs to be picked up. Sometimes, you could be your enemy's motivation. Can you imagine a world where there is no hate? Everyone understands there's a story that makes every person unique. Yet, we relate because we are all humans and need the sun. No matter your skin color, background, or lifestyle, without the sun we all would be dead. Imagine being in a world that actually acknowledges those real-life realities and accepts that we all breathe the same air. We all live under the same sun. Imagine if those realities were put in front of us every day and we could look past the surface of a person. This would be the ideal world where people weren't judged, bullied, or talked about. People would have sympathy towards your situations and would come around to give you words of encouragement. If you could just be yourself, then we could all be free. All the walls would come down and we would be who we were created to be, not what society tells us we should be. We shouldn't care about being accepted and blending in with everyone else. In order to get an opportunity, they tell you to act a certain way. Instead, we would accept that everyone's thumbprint is different. We would be more sensitive to people's hurt, pains and sorrow. Imagine a world that embraced your success.

CHAPTER 9
WHY HATE WON'T DIE

Hate is a feeling so intense or enthusiastic it can move individuals to act on their most savage intentions. We were all taught that this word HATE is strong and powerful and that it should not be thrown around loosely. Why is hate so powerful? Why does hate awaken the worst in individuals? Hate is based on your perspective and overall life experiences that can cause you to feel great malice and disgust towards a person. This can consume your thoughts, and make your actions become fueled with hate. Hatred can trigger parts of the brain responsible for planning and execution, it can drive an individual to demonstrate thoughts or actions that are not normal to their character. Hate is something to be feared, as it can cause harmful or even fatal outcomes for the hated party. Bias is a known motive that promotes hate. It usually starts with hating a race, gender, religious group, or someone's sexual orientation etc. Extreme disgust, fear, and anger are all motivations of hate, depending on someone's background and life or trauma experiences. Bias is a large factor that can cause unfair judgment against a certain individual or group of people. Bias, just like hate, if not tamed will simply grow into something so monstrous that it cannot be controlled. After a while the behavior becomes normal and a baseline for the individual, so now in their mind it is right, it becomes a part of their character. Hate can move to various levels, for example threats, violence, or fatal acts if there is no regulation of sorts. Hate is often a learned behavior that can be passed on generationally. For example, prejudice is a preconceived notion that does not come from facts or experiences but more from assumptions. There are families in which children are taught to hate a person or group of people for whatever targeted reason. As those children get older, they can and will form their own experiences. There are some individuals that will unfortunately stick with their preconceived thoughts due to their upbringing. This notion can cause fear for those who are prejudiced because they never really experienced that group of people they have prejudged. Anger, disgust, animosity, insecurity and other emotions are usually short-lived emotions, but hate is more permanent and an ongoing emotion. Hatred takes great focus and energy, and it will consume and overpower the thoughts of that individual to a point of fixation. Hate and rage are apparent in all humans, meaning we are all equipped with those emotions, but will we all act on those emotions? No. There are individuals who are impulsive, and who therefore can and will act on the hate that they feel no matter their reasoning for it. This does not mean that they are crazy or unhinged, but we as people are not wired the same way or certain stimuli may not affect one person the way it affects the other. What I can react to may not motivate you to act on. We must consider this when interacting with individuals and how we can come off or are perceived. At times we move or say things unintentionally, without regard to how that can harm or penetrate the thoughts or actions of others. This is an effortless way to motivate the hate in others due to emotional reactions based on judgment.

CHAPTER 10
THE DANGERS OF HATE

Does envy play a direct role in fomenting hate? Envy is feeling discontented and being full of resentment. It is characterized by focusing on what others have. Have you ever envied someone else's material belongings, or the dream job, or that happy family—even though what they present may not be what it seems? I believe every one of us has had that feeling before, no matter how successful or positive we may be. Have you ever felt that someone you knew did not deserve that promotion? These are the questions we find ourselves asking. Now this does not turn into hate for everyone. For some, it is just a quick emotion that they can overcome; but others unfortunately cannot. There are individuals who are malicious, and will take envy and turn it into anger. It is human to compare ourselves to other people, but that can spiral into different intensities of envy and hatred.

Anger is another motivation of hate; it can potentially lead to disloyalty in different relationships. The variable of anger can be constant within hate. How? Well, look at it this way: both anger and hate are negative emotions, and in times of anger the feelings you have towards someone can snowball into hate. Anger typically is an emotion that does not last, in contrast to hate, which is more long lasting. Once the emotion of hatred is built up, it can be irreversible and in some cases can span a lifetime. There have been unique cases where hate can be passed through generations and infiltrate the mind and of course the impulses of humans. I want you to reflect on a time where you were at your angriest. How did your body feel, and what were your thoughts at that time? Were you able to control your thoughts or were they scattered? Most probably will not remember how they felt in that instance due to the increase of adrenaline, but you will remember what or who caused that anger. Anger is the strongest emotion that can fuel hatred. We must make sure our thoughts are lateral in those moments and we are thinking before we act.

So, let us get to it! Why do we as people hate others? Is it due to envy or jealousy, or are we just miserable with ourselves and do not know how to deal with it? Is it projecting the feelings of our unhappy selves onto others? Hate can be caused due to feelings of envy, focusing on what others have, whether it be good looks, riches, or just them being well liked. There are times that people will say they are happy with themselves, but we must realize that we all seek perfection within ourselves, so we tend to be our own worst critics and begin comparing ourselves to others. The unfortunate truth of this is that we will never get to a level of perfection, because we simply are not and will never be that. The emotion of hate can indicate that we may lack something within ourselves that we see in someone else. So this again represents a case of looking at our shortcomings and comparing ourselves to others. The feeling of someone being inferior to you can conjure hate. You thinking someone is smarter than you or vice versa can cause a feeling of hatred. This can contribute to your insecurity, the feeling you can never measure up, or feeling just not "good enough." There could be a trigger from childhood trauma or from a parent or specific event. Not receiving the proper praise, or lack of praise growing up can add to those feelings. This will increase envious feelings towards those you consider to be higher than yourself. Consider this: individuals may have hatred that has stemmed from other forms of trauma, for example embarrassment or humiliation.

CHAPTER 11
THE HATE IS BIGGER THAN YOU

Another perspective of how hatred is developed is based on this quote "misery loves company." Now that we have heard this time after time, let us dive into this concept more. At times, people can come together and connect due to shared hatred of another individual. This can generate shared negative thoughts on views directed towards their target. If they see that slander paying off, this just causes the hate to brew more. People need someone to project their negative energy onto, also known as a "scapegoat." Then there is a way to place blame on someone else rather than face their problems and reflect on what is causing them the anger. Individuals who are unhappy can be a dangerous force to be reckoned with. For example, they are so unhappy they want others to feel that same emotion. What are the common reasons for hate to happen? It can be based on unhappiness within the home, at work, and even relationships. In order to not feel alone and isolated, or submerged in their hate, making others feel miserable gives people great delight. In a way they are fixated on making others feel as horrible as them, so it influences the negative behaviors.

HATE... is it the hate of thyself? Are the things that we hate or fear our reflections of self? Is this the reason we may project that on others? When Sigmund Freud spoke about projection, he pointed out that we reject things we may not like about ourselves, and that causes us to outwardly attack others. The problem with that is, if we never find our peace, that outward hate and projection will more than likely continue. In most cases hate may cause us to avoid the individuals that trigger our projection, to protect our peace, happiness, success, or wellbeing. Many of us look at hate always in a negative light, but we must also realize we may hate people who we fear. We may feel that this person that we have strong hate towards may threaten all those things listed above. There are individuals who have been through childhood traumas, or victims of kidnapping, domestic violence, and rape. This fear will cause anxieties of all forms that can contribute to our hate, because they form our triggers. Victims of those types of abuse may look at someone and may be triggered because the color of their skin may match their attacker, or even their smile, scent or other resemblances can trigger PTSD. Often, we may not remember that hate is sometimes just due to our experiences and the nature of the beast; it's undeniable. If it has the potential to hurt us, we will always try to avoid those things by any means necessary. If it causes any type of discomfort, especially psychological discomfort, we will avoid it to refrain from anger that can turn into hatred. Pain avoidance is necessary and must be acknowledged when we speak of hatred in our truest human form. Anything that may cause potential harm and make us fearful, we will try to avoid at any cost. Sometimes when we feel threatened, our fear can transform into hatred and lead to actions. They are permanent to protect ourselves from that harm.

CHAPTER 12
THE FUEL

Jealousy and hatred are two closely related mechanisms. The thought of watching someone accomplish things that you feel you are not able to can lead to hatred. Diving deeper into this theory, the fact that they can do something so great, and the thought that you are not able to, can expose the hatred. As individuals, we are all gifted, but sometimes those gifts are unseen to ourselves. We tend to focus on the things we cannot do rather than the things in which we are gifted. A person will focus on the gifts of others, which can turn into great hatred. The hatred will lead to talks or criticism, but will add to that person's insecurity. The hatred just steamrolls into something greater, but for the worst. It is important to acknowledge that hate is one thing, but its growth can lead individuals to a world of trouble that cannot be changed after hurt and pain is inflicted. Hate breeds even more hate; the harboring of such feelings does not end well, especially for negative emotions. Individuals who direct hate towards another person are lonely and seeking any form of attention, whether negative or positive. It is easy for individuals to sit back and add fuel to a fire, which may be effortless for them to do. This goes back to the notion of coming together to form or increase hate with another individual, for example a hate group. Again, misery loves company: when it comes to negativity and hate, it is easy to find allies because, unfortunately, we as humans focus more on the negative than the positive. The world thrives off negative news or the downfall of individuals. If a person is successful, it is like the world loves a downfall and then a comeback story, it is just society. Hate can form new bonds or strengthen those existing bonds to direct hate towards another person or group. Insecurity and hate also have a deep relation to this. When we present hatred it will emerge. Comparing yourself to other individuals will feed into the delusion and again cause projection to explain away their anxieties. At times, our lack of power can make us feel that we hate another person—again projecting. An example of this may be bullying and again victims of abuse. The longer a person is in a defenseless state, the likelihood of them erupting is undeniable when they can no longer withstand that abuse by another. Eventually something will happen to end this abuse, and an attack due to hatred or fear of this individual is inevitable.

CHAPTER 13
HOW HATE IS ENCOURAGED

Instagram, Facebook, Twitter, and other social media have shown us all diverse ways of envy, jealousy, and overall attention-seeking behaviors that may fuel our hatred of people we have never met. Unfortunately, hate thrives on many social media platforms and has opened a new dynamic on how we judge others. We as people will look at what we perceive and start to compare our lives to it, for the good or the bad. Some will feel inferior to it and others may judge, feeling that they are better than those they view on platforms. The problem with that is people rarely show the negative aspects of their lives in a post, not glorifying their pitfalls and natural human obstacles. We can get caught up in the "grass is greener" aspect, not understanding how those individuals we hate may not be living the life we see them post. On social media we can create our own false reality and perspectives. People must keep this in mind before acting to hate personalities due to how they post.

Racism as well as hate speech is now a problem on social media, including bullying, and it causes easy targets for hate. In one aspect, we see the glitz and glamour or the "relationship goals" and hate that individual for flaunting this. We often see that they are in a sense "winning" at everything and it is pushed to the forefront and in your face daily. Too many users describe the internet as overwhelming and frustrating. Because we are force-fed posts and stories, many individuals including celebs have reported it plays significantly on their emotions. Hate and hate groups thrive on social media platforms and can now spread hate faster and more effectively than ever before. We must consider regulating the time we spend on social media and being self-aware of the things we view. We also need to make sure the algorithms fit the things we want to see, which make us happy, and not necessarily things that trigger our envy and jealousy. The world is connected in every way. We spend most of our lives scrolling and comparing, and this will affect or trigger insecurities, self-image, and self-worth dramatically. Online hate speech has been severely directed towards individuals due to their sexual orientation. They are targeted and attacked, ridiculed and more due to who they choose to identify as or who to love. Platforms try to have guidelines and restrictions to filter and end hate speech online, but this does not eliminate the problem. In the last few years, there have been laws set up to make those attacks hate crimes, but we still have a long way to go to keep up with the ever-changing internet.

We have accepted that technology has added to our lives in regard to social media, but we have also seen fear, hate and envy grow because of toxic viewpoints.

Judging others and hate has a common relationship as well. Why? We all have it in us to hate, judge, and hold jealousy. We all have natural human emotions within us that I am sure most, including myself, may not want to admit. It's more like if we were put in certain situations that may identify and uncover our hatred, what are we capable of doing? There is no way to really know unless there is something, someone or an event that awakens that emotion. In a sense, it may lay dormant. We can never imagine being put in a situation where you or someone you love has been done harm. That harm can create great pain and hatred. Often, someone may remind you of a failure, and once again may create doubts. In turn, projection of hate may be directed towards that person.

There are a multitude of reasons as to why people hate others, and as life continues, we will be likely to reveal more reasons. There will be encounters that we face that will shape our thoughts and experiences that have the chance of becoming hatred. This hatred can be towards yourself or be projected. Please consider how hatred can be detrimental to you and even affect your thoughts and health regarding stress. Self-reflection to probe and understand your feelings is healthy and beneficial, not just for self but when it comes to interacting in a diverse world.

CHAPTER 14
REMOVE THE STATE OF CONDITIONING

Conditioning is the process of training or accustoming a person or animal to behave in a certain way or to accept certain circumstances. We begin to be conditioned at a very young age. This could be from our environment or simply from watching television. Either way, some of the information we take in is not always good. What we learn from childhood can contribute to the hate people portray or experience from these conditions. Those scenarios can shape our perception of life as we get older. For example, watching television as a child can train you to think certain types of people are bad or dangerous, while other types of people are good or pure. These conditions can cause you to create stereotypes. This is also apparent when you hear information in the news about some cities or states having high crime rates. As that information is taken in, it creates a mind to judge people in those particular areas. Now, when you meet a person living in an impoverished community, you will immediately revert back to those statistics. This will cause you to believe that information, create a false perception of people in those communities, then treat them accordingly.

In order to remove the hate, jealousy, rage, and stereotypes, you must restore the thoughts in your mind to break down the conditioning. You must start afresh and re-educate yourself on what you thought you knew. Begin reading new books to expand your vocabulary. Learn to accept that everyone has a story. Although some people have had different circumstances than others, everyone should be viewed equally. Anyone can get hit with a life-changing experience at any moment. Try to do research from a state of understanding other people, not from a judgmental standpoint. This is how you truly get to know people, and understand how conditioning makes people display certain behaviors, affect their decision making, and impact their perceptions in life.

Some people hate because you have things they want or envy. They believe you are attached to something that will give them value or a greater identity. When these particular people don't have the same possessions, it grieves their heart. They have convinced themselves that owning the same materials or status will make their world better. In addition, their emotions are attached to getting the praise you receive from being in your position of success. They're not after the material things, they're after the praise from the fame or notoriety. This is because there was some sort of neglect at some point in their life. Maybe they had that dream job and lost it, or maybe they felt unappreciated for something major they did. This causes them to go through life observing people and finding ways to make them feel more valuable.

CHAPTER 15
ADDICTIONS

When you are on top of the world and everyone worships you, those chemicals boost your adrenaline and send signals to the brain that feel good. This is similar to the high people chase when they are under any form of addiction. This can even produce a chain reaction if they were once that person in your position, but things aren't working in their favor at the moment. This can put them in a space of regret and channel a series of emotions. Hate isn't always about someone not liking you; sometimes a person has internal problems that have nothing to do with you. However, you may be the person they are paying attention to when reflecting on themselves. They have now begun to create this image of you as a mini-god in their mind. They start to worship you without even realizing it. When idolizing you brings no benefit to them, that worship then evolves into envy, and then into hate. Everyone has different addictions. Some people are addicted to attention and achievements, just as the next person is addicted to drugs. The result will be the same if they can't get their high, which can cause them to do crazy stuff. It's the same as a person who sits on Instagram all day looking at other people's profiles and comparing their lives to their own lives. If they are not strong in their conscious mind, then it can lead to people demonstrating actions unconsciously. This can lead to dangerous actions because you're operating in a different world and are out of touch with reality. It is important to be fully aware of the reality you live in, so those emotions don't transpire to others negatively.

After years in the entertainment industry, I realized how many influencers I worked with didn't love themselves. They projected love on social media, but behind closed doors it was false advertisement. I've seen celebrity couples break up. One person leaves their partner at the height of their career. Instead of manifesting that pain into paychecks, they allowed the hurt to block them from greater opportunities. They became the headline of the one left behind versus the one who broke free and discovered their purpose. I was right there every step of the way trying to keep them focused, but they would quit business deals before giving them time to flourish. I realized they were in the spotlight with everyone looking at their every move, hoping for the worst while their family was being torn apart. Everyone wanted to know what they were going to do next, while their ex-partner was blowing up. Instead of using the momentum to get ahead, it manifested into hate and caused that person to become distracted. Instead of closing and fulfilling contract deals, they became content in their pain while their former lover thrived in their own individuality.

CHAPTER 16
NEGATIVITY

While many people discuss negative outcomes, no one acknowledges where that negativity comes from. Every person is born with a fresh start, full of hope and vibrancy. Unfortunately, our personality gets tainted when negativity is introduced into our world through experiences in our upbringing. This can cause your mind to absorb different responses and manifest through your behavior, forms of communication, and interaction with people overall. That perception is no longer pure. The DNA and inner workings of a person will determine how negative experiences will affect them. People are exposed to negativity through conversations, media, and other people's viewpoints. Negativity is handed down to children. Although kids at certain ages can't verbally express themselves and tell their parents when they're being negative, they can physically express it through their actions. Your negativity literally changes your children. This is why no one is born hating people; they are taught hate through hateful experiences, proving hate is a learned behavior that can be unlearned.

Sometimes, we can grow up in broken homes with dysfunctional parents. The child doesn't understand why their life is the way it is. They just know this is what they go through and how they live every day. If they live like this for a series of years, they might think it's normal, because it's all they know. Some children were exposed to their parents being high on drugs all the time.

Some parents might have left their children with pedophiles as babysitters, and they thought it was normal to let someone touch them inappropriately. Some parents might have been prostitutes and exposed their children to their sexual behaviors. Some parents were violent towards each other and fought in front of their children. Some parents were prejudiced and spoke racial slurs in their homes about people who didn't look like them. All this while, the child was soaking up everything and being groomed to think it's normal. As the child gets older and begins to engage in romantic relationships, they either repeat the same cycle or they make a commitment to not end up how their parents were. Some of those individuals, who are now adults, probably promised to never put their children through that same stress and to give them better, to ensure their child grows up in a healthy, two-parent household. But what happens when that commitment is broken? I've seen it many times. One parent develops hate towards the other parent because they feel like it's their fault for breaking their promise to themselves. It can foster resentment towards the significant other to think you both can't get on the same page because you don't feel seen or heard. It can lead one person to say things that are hard to come back from, because of the frustration of feeling like you can't both get on one accord. Now, you have to process the idea of becoming a statistic in being labeled as a single parent. It changes how you treat that child, because you feel like you've already failed before even beginning the parenthood journey. You start to believe you could never give your child what you always promised you would do for them before they were even born. That perfect picture of showing them what it's like to grow up in a loving home where the parents love and like each other. That desire to give your child access to a healthy balance of masculine and feminine energy simultaneously under one roof. Sometimes hate can brew in these situations, because you want the love so badly and resent the person for not giving it to you. The child is now developing in the womb, taking on all this energy. The child is unconsciously developing anger and malice in their little beating heart without understanding why. Then as the child grows up, you're trying to understand why the child has negative outbursts, a bad attitude, or disciplinary issues in school. This is the result of these negative emotions that weren't controlled and reverted into negative energy while in the womb. Sometimes we get caught up in the deliverer but forget about the package. It's not the delivery guy or the woman being the host, it's about the package you've been waiting on. The delivery guy is the man providing the fertilization. The package is the development and arrival of the baby in the physical form. The host is the woman chosen to receive the package. When we get distracted from wanting the relationship with the significant other to be a certain way, we tend to forget about the blessing from the birth of the child arriving safely with a sound mind. Instead, we tend to see how the lack of these desires fulfilled can make you hate the person who is giving and receiving the package. There's no need to hate that person. Maybe their mission was greater than what you see presently. Maybe they were supposed to be just the delivery guy or the host at that moment. Maybe if you didn't intertwine with that person to create life, you would have lost your life in the midst of living life. Let's think about how many people let circumstances beat the life out of them while walking around in their body lifeless. They have no motivation and no drive, just waking up every day to repeat the same cycle. It's one thing to create life, but the hardest thing is to keep life in you. Many people literally live their whole life fighting to keep their life going. Remember that negative emotions are distractions to keep you from enjoying and properly utilizing your gifts. More energy is required to hate someone than to be the person who leads with love. When you know better, you do better, so our children can live better. A lot of people are hurting from their parents' mistakes. We have to make a commitment to stop the traumatic domino effect, because it makes the future more complicated. This is how trauma is passed from generation to generation.

CHAPTER 17
FRUSTRATION

Everyone wonders why famous people get murdered in their own hometown. You would think this is where you can be yourself and more relaxed, but the truth is home is where you receive the most hate. These are the people who come from your same neighborhood and grew up with you.

When things don't work for that person, their frustration manifests into something more. It becomes an internal problem because they had the same potential and opportunities to decide what they wanted to produce in their life. Of course, there are unforeseen situations that take place or certain challenges arise, but the difference between you and them is their decision to quit at some point. Then when that person continues to grow and blow up, that person from your hometown will remember you from the beginning while the world sees you for your accomplishments. So when someone sees you experience success in real time and watches you go from zero to one hundred, the frustration sets in and produces regret. They begin to question why this person made it and they didn't. Then the regret transforms into anger. Maybe they regret not staying friends with you. Maybe they regret the times in high school when they didn't believe in you when you were younger, when you performed at the school talent shows or started your business. It's always hard for people to believe in something that hasn't happened yet. It's because they don't see your vision. By the time everything comes into fruition, the world gets to see the finished product and love you, even though they weren't there to experience you from the bottom. However, the people who do experience you from the bottom have a different perspective of you. They feel a sense of entitlement even if they didn't contribute to your success. This is because you both started off at the same place, so they think you both should meet at the finish line together. When that doesn't happen, people tend to take your success personally. This is usually because there is an emotional attachment that is either functional or dysfunctional. They begin to want to be like you, since they feel like you're both the same. If you spend so much time wanting to be like someone else, then who's going to be you? People actually put it in their mind that it's necessary to obtain what you have. They don't even know who they are anymore, because they are seeking their identity through you. It becomes hard to escape you when they hear you everywhere, like your music on the radio or your business mentioned in the news media. Now all they are stuck with are the memories, telling stories of early days to proclaim this person as their only way out. Now if they can't have what you have, that regret of not pursuing their dreams turns into animosity, which now evolves into hate. They want it so bad that if they can't have it, then they feel nobody else should have it either. Those emotions they're experiencing within themselves persuades them to make an executive decision to take it away from you because they don't have it. I believe people do harm to other people because they want to stop them from furthering their growth. They start to question why they didn't make it if you both came from the same place. People who are not from your hometown don't feel this way, because they never knew you. So, there's no sense of entitlement or feeling like you owe them something due to your success, because there is no personal connection. Celebrities receive the most hate in their hometown because you were once one of them. So when they see you on television becoming famous, those emotional attachments are activated. It's true, you won't always remain friends with the people you met in grade school. Yet, any amount of time spent with someone in the past can make people think you owe them when you make it. Even if you haven't talked to that person in ten years, they'll say, "Remember when we used to…" That's a sign they are trying to get you to feel like they had some type of contribution to your life, as if the time they spent with you was so valuable. When you don't give them the credit they feel they deserve, they feel a sense of betrayal. Now you'll hear them say, "You act like you don't know anybody anymore…" They feel like if they are struggling and you are rich, then you have to be stopped. You must realize that people are competitive. You have to blow up in your city first before you blow up in other markets. So when you blow up, you become this hometown hero that everyone is rooting for. When you go national, now it's a problem, because now you are not accessible. When you're off the radar for so long and finally come back home, that's their only opportunity to bring destruction into your life, because they feel they can reach you. They meet you at the core of your foundation. This is why going back to your own community after making it can be very dangerous, because you're going back to old relationships. This could be reminders of break ups, old high school beef you thought was over, or people that knew you when you were struggling and offered you money. No one cares when you don't make it, yet people will remember the time they shared with you when you make it, no matter if it was good or bad. Depending on how they feel about their life will determine how they will react about yours.

CHAPTER 18
THINGS TO REMEMBER

When you start to feel that negative self-talk coming about yourself and others, here's what you should consider.

1. Everything will work out for you in perfect timing.

2. If you're trying to be someone else, then who will be you?

3. There is no benefit in wanting what someone else has, what's for you will be for you.

4. You have today, yesterday is over, make the most of the moment.

5. It's never too late to start over.

6. If you only know what pain that person had to go through to get to the top, you would see them so differently.

7. Your feelings and emotions are controlled by your experiences; don't let them fool you.

8. "Dark cannot drive out darkness; only light can do that." ~ Dr. Martin Luther King, Jr.

9. Sometimes we all feel down in the dumps. It's normal; it's called life.

10. Give it one more try.

11. Comparing your life to others will get you nothing but a headache. You're special in your own way.

12. We are all actors, but some of us are better at it. Life looks really perfect on social media.

13. Social media is not real, it's a program that we manipulate to post what we believe people will love us for.

14. You are good enough.

15. The small things in your life have the most value.

16. Your thought life wants to control your reality. Be careful: the mind is very powerful.

17. It's ok, it is what it is.

18. Don't quit. If that direction does not work, go another way.

19. Everyone's journey is different.

20. Make peace with yesterday and focus on the future.

21. Never give up. One step a day is still progress.

22. Trust me: there will be more opportunities, but it's up to you to stay in the game called life.

23. You cannot go back in time and erase the beginning, but you can pick up where you are and change the outcome.

24. Nothing that is meant for you will pass you by (medium.com).

25. "Most people see what is and never see what can be" ~ Albert Einstein.

26. You got up this morning. Before you start your day, just remember: someone didn't get up.

27. Everything you need is inside you.

28. Things may not have gone the way you planned, but they will go the way they should in the long haul.

29. Your age is just a number, not a roadblock. Don't get the two confused.

30. You're different, enjoy it. There is not a box big enough that everyone can fit in. Some people just gotta stay outside the box.

31. All it takes is one opportunity.

32. Someone will love you, just give it time. Maybe that special person is coming out of a breakthrough (not a "break up"), and will be made perfect for you. You see other people happy, but just remember they have a story too.

CHAPTER 19
IT'S LIFE

We are born into this world clear of mental blockages. Every person is given the opportunity to live fully and order the steps of their path. However, it is the encounter with unfortunate situations that alters our original shape. It's the experience of traumas in your childhood that determines how you spend your adulthood. Many of us get trapped into the concept of paying for psychologists to heal from the hurt and let-downs we've experienced when we were young. There are many people who were born so brilliant, yet negative situations sent them down a different path. These same people years later are called names like crazy or evil, but we forget about the damage that was done that caused them to take their life in a different direction. While many of us wish we could pick our parents, it's just not the way we were designed. I'm sure if we could, everyone would pick their ideal life. Instead, we live in a world where some parents instill hate and project their beliefs onto their child. Some families even practice hate and are placed in scenarios that groom a hateful personality. Since life is out of our hands, we can only hope that children are born to good parents and have a decent upbringing. It's like gambling with a deck of cards that determines how your life will look.

Never forget, the core of the root of hate is jealousy. When a person is content or comfortable with themselves, they don't really desire to be like other people. They are really happy with how their life is and are genuinely happy for someone else's blessings or success. It's called appreciating who you are. People who are insecure and unhappy with their lives are inclined to hate you. When someone is jealous of you, they feel a deep desire to shut you down. This is because their perspective is fogged by their own misery, and they will see you as a threat. It's hard for these people to admit they are wrong, because they believe that is a sign of weakness. Insecurities and vulnerability lead people to seek to destroy who you are in order to feel better about themselves. You threaten their beliefs and expose who they truly are on the inside. But remember: a person who feels inferior can never take a powerhouse down.

In addition, never underestimate the power of frustration. What happens to us emotionally affects our body and mind. Frustration can come from something failing over and over again, which makes it hard to see the possibility of those results. Those good emotions, optimism and excitement are destroyed from frustration and cause you to lose hope for the future. You then lose confidence, develop stress, experience anger, sadness or even rage. This can cause your body to have a negative reaction if your mind has already decided that something is being blocked. It's just like being in a bad relationship. You feel stuck or feel like you can't walk away from a person. You become frustrated, which then could lead to aggressive behavior. Some people in this position may start doing crazy things, which now makes them a dangerous person. Maybe you're not being treated the way you desire, or you're not growing in the relationship, or don't feel fulfilled with the person you're with. This frustration can sometimes turn into resentment if the person on the receiving end feels like you're holding them back. On the contrary, maybe somebody had a goal of having a successful marriage because they grew up in a dysfunctional home. So when the relationship starts to go downhill, that deep rooted trauma triggers them to spaz out. Maybe they saw their parents arguing their whole life, so they promised themselves to be a better example of "relationship goals." All in all, you never know what's attached to that let down of that desired achievement.

Society teaches us to overlook the damaging effects of things not going according to plan. We often take these things for granted and do not acknowledge the seriousness of when someone falls into a state of frustration. These things can include the dissatisfaction of a job or inequality in the world. Oftentimes, people are taught to tough it out or get over it. At some point, we have to change how we feel about frustration and how we allow it to affect us. It's not bad to get frustrated, because it lets us know when something is wrong. However, it's important to get help so you don't avoid those emotions and allow them to block you from your desired outcomes. Use this as motivation to make changes to achieve your goals no matter what. Stress will only weigh down on your body and affect the rest of your years to come, such as your sleeping patterns, eating habits, and interpersonal skills. Stress can also affect the way you feel about and see yourself. This can lead to self-destructive behaviors, like developing addictions to alcohol or drugs. Unfortunately, many people self-medicate to deal with their frustrations. So, when you encounter cold-hearted people in your life, know there is an internal battle going on that doesn't have anything to do with the person they are hating. This person has convinced themselves that no one is deserving of luxuries if they don't have it, without even understanding what that person went through to achieve such success.

CHAPTER 20
NEGATIVE SELF-TALK

We all have a little voice in our head that tells us what to do. Most haters all have that negative voice in their head to antagonize them making them feel like another person has achieved something they could never have. That little voice can make you believe you don't have something special about yourself, that someone is better than everyone else, that it's okay to gossip about someone. Sometimes, our thoughts can be our biggest enemy and alter our reality. At some point, you have to turn that voice off and say, "It's not real." Some negative self-talk is attached to the brainwashing you experienced growing up against your own will, such as from watching television, or conversations embedded into your mind. I've been blessed to have the opportunity to lend a helping hand in many talented individuals' careers. I remember working with an artist who had to practice patience for many years. They signed a music deal with one of the hottest management groups and were confident their life was going to go to the top in no time. Shortly after signing their deal, an artist signed before them dropped the hit of their career and took off. The industry was loving this person so much that the management team began investing more time into their music to maintain the momentum. While it was a great look for the company to have all these platinum and gold plaques and chart-topping songs under their belt, it pushed the newly signed artist further to the back of the line. Now this person had to watch someone get their claim to fame right before their eyes while being put on the backburner. Before they knew it, years had gone by and still didn't yield the same results as they were hoping for. That disappointment could have easily led them to hate the person who they could have felt was stealing their shine. Instead of letting the negative self-talk consume their mind, they disciplined themselves, practiced self-love, and focused on perfecting their craft. Instead of hating the person, they started to study them to strengthen their brand and platform. That person became their motivation, instead of their public enemy. Sometimes, you have to practice discipline in the midst of your pain in order to reap the benefits. Sometimes, you simply have to wait your turn. The moment you hear that little voice being negative, you have to realize it's a trap to keep you from elevating. Don't let that voice convince you that something is taking too long, so maybe you should give up. It's important to have a clear understanding of your reality, so that dark energy doesn't give birth to animosity towards someone that isn't the problem to begin with.

Hate can be connected to the experiences of your youth that have shaped your subconscious mind. Maybe you got into an argument with someone. Maybe your personality and attitude is a result of when someone gets you upset or you have a bad experience. Sometimes, we are dealing with trauma that we've masked for so long and now we're dealing with the regrets. When doing so, it can present itself as if it's the end of the world for you and it puts you in a funk. At some point, there has to be a solution to the "if I can't have it, you can't have it" syndrome. This has caused many crimes, causing families to go through pain as a result of this negative emotion. Hate can cause you to become overly competitive. Maybe your parents made you feel like a loser if you didn't win every game. Maybe they made you feel like less of a person if you didn't meet their standards. As an adult, you are carrying this same weight on your shoulders because of the fearful emotions instilled into you. You grow up seeing life as one big competition, and it all started from your horrible parents. So you don't go through life living it, you go through life competing with it. When you can't have it your way, all hell breaks loose. We see it on social media where women try to outdo one another. They try to have the best body to be considered the baddest chick. It's to the point that people are willing to do anything to be number one. Why can you not want to be better just because that's what you want to do? Why can we not take the competitiveness out of everything? At some point, it gets dangerous. We see it all the time in political party campaigns. Each candidate tries to dish out as much defamatory information on the other candidate to make themselves appear more righteous. It's not even about the people, it's about who can get the most votes by getting the people to hate the less favorable party. It's the "crab in a barrel" mentality, when people see life as one big competition. This is a problem no one is talking about.

CHAPTER 21
POT BOILING

Hate is almost impossible to avoid in life because there's a psychology behind the emotion. Hate can stem from low self-esteem, financial insecurities, lack of meaningful accomplishments, or the need to project one's flaws onto someone else. While it is never deserved, you can't help that there will be people who feel inferior to your success. Social media makes it so easy to feel hate towards someone because everyone looks like they're living a better life than the next person. When people post mean comments, it's like a mini escape from their reality. It's a sense of empowerment because they feel like they're saying what everyone else is thinking, when indeed it's probably just them alone. The truth is: we are influenced by the people we are closest to or value most. Comparing yourself to other people can make you feel uncertain about the direction of your life. Uncertainty can breed worry and cause you to explode. When you feel that sense of dissatisfaction with life creeping up, you can either work to eliminate it, choose to live with it, or actively hate on the people living the life you want. At the end of the day, you have to take accountability for your decisions and live with it. I think about people like my cousin who's sitting in prison to this day. He grew up in the projects with a crackhead as a father. He didn't deserve to grow up like that, but it was the deck of cards he was dealt. He could have played his hand anyway he liked. That could have included using his parents as an example of what not to be like. He could have actively taken control of his life and used it as motivation to be more than what his environment offered. He could have reached out to anybody to get guidance on the direction of his life. Instead, he became a victim of his environment and fell into the trap of the streets to justify the hate in his heart. While his parents played a huge role in his upbringing, he chose to stay in his suffering rather than to seek the proper resources. You have to believe in your subconscious mind that you're going to be fine.

I didn't write this book to spotlight people who've been wronged or families that've been humiliated by hateful crimes. I also didn't write this book to ask people to understand a criminal. My objective for this book was to provide a genuine understanding of the emotions that drive hateful intentions from my perception and through research. I believe that haters are your biggest fans, and they can disguise themselves as righteous individuals. Some people argue that if you don't have any haters then you're not doing enough. My hope is for people to reach out to different help groups, community organizations, and utilize the mental health resources available to overcome the experiences of hate. I want people to know they don't have to be a pot sitting for years with water boiling in your mind until it gets so hot and spills over. My objective is to help people before it's too late. These people tend to seek revenge and want to hurt someone because they're so passionate about the pain they've experienced. It's okay to get help. Going to jail for hurting people is not the answer and is no way to live your life. You don't want to put yourself in a situation where you throw your whole life away. Although you may be done unfairly, there are better ways to stand up for yourself. We see it all the time. People get so overwhelmed that they begin to self-destruct. We hear it all the time in the media about innocent people getting killed at mass shootings and cars rushing through large crowds, all because of hate. Hurt only produces more frustrations. Sometimes an intervention is necessary to save your own life.

When I wrote my first book *Give It One More Try*, I was hurt. It took a lot of faith to get to a point of not hating my group members after we lost our record deal. We had a lot of money on the line and lost it all in a split second because of someone else's personal issues. It took a lot of growing and self-development for me not to want to hit them in the face every time I saw them. I was upset for a while because I felt like a failure. It took a lot of consistency in changing my perspective on why everything happened. I had to destroy the victim mentality in order not to fall into the hate trap. Reading relaxation and stress books blocked me from traveling down a hateful road. There is power in books. When you read books, your eyes are opened to a whole new world from someone else's lenses. It helped me release grudges towards my brothers and other people who've done me wrong. Even to this day, I continue to fight those urges against people who've tried to stop the success in my life right now. I've had people try to mess up my name by destroying my character with lies. I've had people try to destroy some of my relationships in the attempt to shatter my career and dreams. When transitioning from an artist to an entrepreneur, I knew the stakes depended highly on my actions. I've worked on so many business deals where I thought I was working with a partner but was truly working with a competitor. They would listen to my ideas and try to sabotage the deal by compromising the client to make themselves appear more favorable while cutting me out of the deal. My partner and I would have television deals on the table, and they would break confidentiality to shop the deal around to secure the highest bidder.

Even when I've tried to help talented celebrities take their career to the next level, I could have known them for years and always had their best interest at heart and in mind, they would still allow outside people with less experience to come into the picture and persuade them to think they had a better idea to steal the client. They wouldn't yield any real results, just a lower price and high hopes for sale. They would ultimately gain the client to drive clout for their brand just to say they worked with them, but not produce real results. After many disappointments, I had to realize that things can backfire on you if a person you're dealing with isn't grounded. Sometimes it's not about getting people to understand you or believe in your dreams, it's about not letting those things destroy your mind when they're happening over and over again. Some people just don't want to see you make it, and you could never change how they feel about it. Don't focus on their actions, focus on how you react to them. I used it as fuel to keep pushing through. I had to make sure that negativity didn't manifest, but merely produce positivity. When doing so, it's also important to think about the consequences that come with acting out of hate. What if I would have punched somebody in the face to prove a point? I would have risked going to jail and messing up my future. You have to adjust when negative energy is being thrown at you. Stress and hate go hand in hand. How you feel in your heart about somebody affects your physical body. Those chemicals entering into your brain are sending a message to your mind, which ultimately gives the other person the power to control the outcomes of your life. Don't lose sight of the bigger picture and become self-centered in your anger. Don't lose sight of the promises you made to yourself, your family, and your dreams. In order to sustain a healthy life, you sometimes have to let some things go, which may include people as well.

CONCLUSION

Negative energy can manifest itself into physical illnesses. It's not worth it to carry negative emotions in your heart and body. When you're being hated in your hometown, it's just a sign that you're excelling in life, doing something they wish they could do, or authentically being yourself. Sometimes, people will hate you when you've never done anything wrong to them. Don't begin to doubt yourself when you experience hate, merely monitor your psychological thoughts and actions. People showcasing inferior emotions towards you are merely suffering on the inside. Until they get help, it's not your responsibility to care about how your success, way of life, financial status, or cultural background makes them feel.

Now that you've read this book, the question is: what are you going to do now? How can you contribute to making things better? While we can't change the entire world, we can better the world around us. What are you going to do about it? How are you going to make a difference? I hope this book has helped you understand a little bit more about hate, why it causes separation in our society, where it comes from, and how we are affected by it. In order for things to get better, it's going to take more people to recognize the seriousness in the awareness of hate and make a decision to do something about it. There is no action too great or small; it starts at home or at work or on social media. No matter where hate is present, you have to commit to do something about it. Whether it's you choosing to work on yourself or finding a way to understand people. It's easy to read this book for understanding, but now it's time to move forward with the information given. Are you going to change your perception of people, or do you even want to? I hope this book helped you to see hate from a different point of view. No one is naturally hateful. Instead, there is something behind the emotion that's been inflicted or programmed. It's time to heal and deprogram how you've been taught to think. It's time to live a new life not fueled by anger or regret, but with a heart of understanding. Just as energy is used to judge and talk about people, use that same energy in a positive way to work on yourself. Develop solutions that contribute to your mind being in a better place when it comes to how you deal with people. We can't save everyone in the world, but we can try to make as much progress as we can. Share this book with your friends or use this as a topic of conversation to break down the mystery of hate.

NOTES

NOTES

NOTES

NOTES

NOTES

NOTES

NOTES

NOTES

NOTES

NOTES

NOTES

NOTES

NOTES

NOTES

NOTES

NOTES

NOTES

NOTES

NOTES

NOTES

www.ingramcontent.com/pod-product-compliance
Lightning Source LLC
Chambersburg PA
CBHW062103270326
41931CB00013B/3189